Peaceful Heroes

JONAH WINTER

illustrated by SEAN ADDY

ARTHUR A. LEVINE BOOKS

AN IMPRINT OF SCHOLASTIC INC.

Introduction

"Hero" is a very old word that comes from Ancient Greece. Back then, over 2,500 years ago, "hero" was a title reserved for warriors who fought to defend their people. These warriors fought with swords and shields, bows and arrows — risking their lives for the sake of their empire or city-state. Songs and poems were written about the bravest of these warriors, celebrating their heroic deeds.

In the modern world, there are still warriors who fight for their people. However, in this modern and very dangerous world of guns and bombs, perhaps we need a different set of heroes to look up to. We need a set of heroes who do not hurt people.

Who are these heroes?

They are firemen who rush into burning buildings to save people.

They are political leaders who risk assassination while fighting injustice through peaceful means.

They are religious leaders who risk their lives preaching messages of love and peace in countries overflowing with hatred and violence.

They are ordinary people doing their best to protect other ordinary people from being killed — *without even using a weapon*.

They would die for their cause, but they would not kill for their cause. They are the modern heroes. They are the *peaceful heroes*.

This book contains just one list of such heroes. There are dozens of lists that could be written. And there are many peaceful heroes among us — parents, friends, and others who have risked their own lives to help other people. Perhaps you could come up with your *own* list of peaceful heroes. . . .

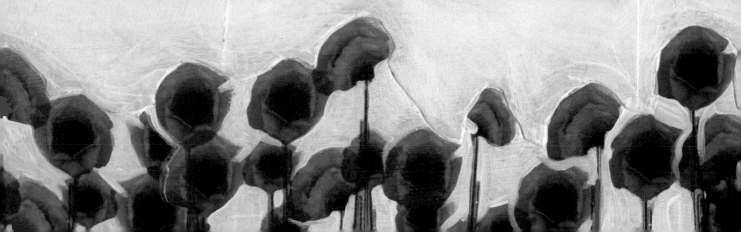

Jesus of Nazareth

(4 BC?– AD 30?)

The world's original peaceful hero is said to have lived 2,000 years ago in Israel, and his name was Jesus of Nazareth. Christians believe that Jesus was and is the Son of God. Muslims believe that Jesus was one of many prophets. Hindus believe that Jesus was a saint, and one of the world's greatest teachers. Jews believe that Jesus existed, but that he was just a man, nothing more. Many people believe that Jesus did not exist at all, and that he is just a myth. But most historians believe that there was indeed a man named Jesus of Nazareth — that he was real.

Whoever Jesus *really* was, his story as told in the Christian Bible provides one of the greatest examples ever of how to be a human being. According to the Christian Bible, Jesus of Nazareth gave his life to helping other people. He healed the sick. He fed the hungry. He protected people threatened by angry mobs. He tried to teach people how to lead better lives, to not hate each other. He devoted much of his life to preaching, and his message was one of love and peace. He said, "Love your neighbor as yourself." He said, "Bless those who curse you." He said, "Love your enemies." He said, "Do good to those who hate you." What a concept! Up to that point in history, everyone thought you were supposed to hate and fight your enemies. But suddenly people were being advised to return hatred with love. If someone slapped your cheek, according to the Jesus of the

Christian Bible, you were not only supposed to take it — you should turn your head and let them slap the other cheek. In other words, you were supposed to respond to evil behavior with good behavior.

These ideas were so new and different that they scared many people — especially the people in charge, for they saw the power in Jesus's way of thinking. It is impossible to fight someone who is unwilling to fight. According to the Christian Bible, Jesus knew that one day he would be killed for being so outspoken, for challenging the accepted ways of thinking, and for challenging the people in power, with their armies and their laws. Nonetheless, he continued preaching and helping people despite the risks. This story, true or not true, has provided the perfect model for peaceful heroes of our time.

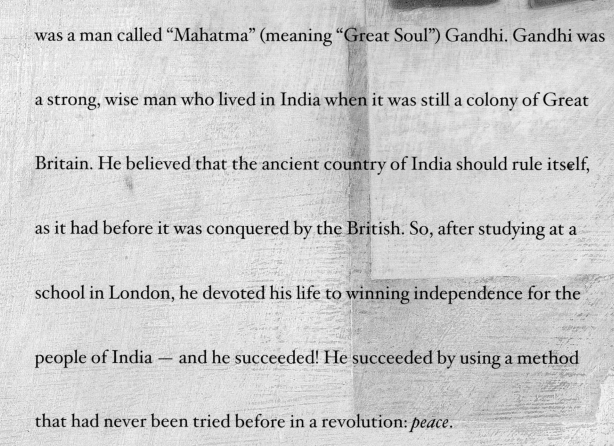

Mahatma Gandhi

(1869-1948)

The first peaceful hero of modern

times to claim Jesus as a role model

was a man called "Mahatma" (meaning "Great Soul") Gandhi. Gandhi was

a strong, wise man who lived in India when it was still a colony of Great

Britain. He believed that the ancient country of India should rule itself,

as it had before it was conquered by the British. So, after studying at a

school in London, he devoted his life to winning independence for the

people of India — and he succeeded! He succeeded by using a method

that had never been tried before in a revolution: *peace*.

Having seen the horrors of modern warfare — guns, tanks, bombs — Gandhi knew that war was not the best method for winning independence. Being a very spiritual man, a Hindu, he also believed that killing people, for whatever reasons, was wrong. Through his spiritual practice, he also knew that all human beings were equal, regardless of how much money they had or what jobs they did. For this reason, he thought that India's class system — in which poor people were called "untouchables" — was just plain wrong, as wrong as violence. So, like Jesus, he himself dressed as a poor person and led a simple life, spending very little money. Dressed in rags, he led his followers on peaceful walks through the streets. He gave powerful speeches. He encouraged all Indians not to pay

no

no

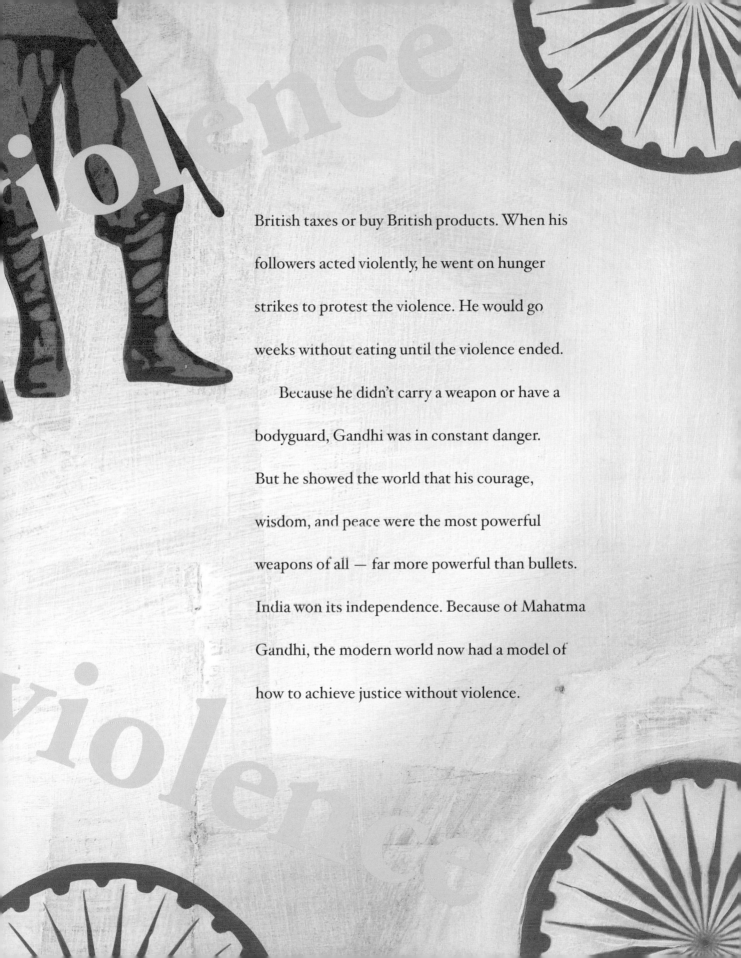

British taxes or buy British products. When his followers acted violently, he went on hunger strikes to protest the violence. He would go weeks without eating until the violence ended.

Because he didn't carry a weapon or have a bodyguard, Gandhi was in constant danger. But he showed the world that his courage, wisdom, and peace were the most powerful weapons of all — far more powerful than bullets. India won its independence. Because of Mahatma Gandhi, the modern world now had a model of how to achieve justice without violence.

Martin Luther King, Jr.

(1929–1968)

Following in the footsteps of Jesus and Gandhi came the greatest of all

American peaceful heroes: the Reverend Dr. Martin Luther King, Jr.

Like Jesus, his first role model, Dr. King devoted his life to preaching

and helping people. He gave powerful

sermons on the topic of racial injustice in America. These sermons were filled with a sense of hope and love. Inspired by the teachings of Jesus, Dr. King encouraged both black and white people to stand up for their own humanity through loving one another.

Like Gandhi, his other role model, Dr. King used the "peaceful demonstration" as a way of combating racism. He knew from Gandhi's example that this method worked. He knew, as Gandhi had known, that peace was the most powerful weapon of all — especially when used by masses of people banding together in public for a common cause. During the 1960s, thousands upon thousands of people marched behind Dr. King as he led them through American cities known for their bigotry and racial injustice. In response to these marches, Dr. King received many, many death threats from angry white people. They wanted to kill him not just for being a black man, but for being a black man that had *the nerve* to

publicly defend his own dignity as a human being. Back then, many white Americans thought that black people should just keep their mouths shut and sit at the back of the bus. Black people were supposed to drink from their own special water fountains, live in their own all-black neighborhoods, and send their children to all-black schools. This, in some states, was *the law*! Like Gandhi, Dr. King encouraged his followers never to resort to violence when confronted by angry white mobs or police dogs or policemen with fire hoses.

Not only was Martin Luther King, Jr., one of the most peaceful, courageous, and selfless men who ever lived, he was largely successful in his mission. Mostly due to his efforts, the *Civil Rights Act* was passed in Congress in 1964, giving people of all races equal rights in America. That same year, Dr. King won the Nobel Peace Prize, a fitting honor for one of history's greatest advocates of peace.

Sojourner Truth

Before there was Martin Luther King, Jr., and the *Civil Rights Act*,

there was the Civil War. And before there was the Civil War, there

was slavery — in the South *and* in the North. And up

north, there was a remarkable woman who began her

life as a slave in New York state.

The name she had as a slave was Isabella Baumfree, which was the name given to her by her Dutch masters. Well, one of the things she did in the years after she won her freedom was to give herself a new name: Sojourner Truth. A "sojourner" is a traveler, and the name seemed to suit her, for as a free woman she traveled all over the North — on foot! — preaching what she knew to be the *truth* against slavery and the racism that caused slavery to happen. And when Sojourner spoke, people listened.

She was a six-foot-tall woman with a barreling voice and a cantankerous disposition. She didn't know how to read, but she had friends read the Bible to her repeatedly, so many times that she had practically memorized it — enough so that she often went into "whites-only" churches and got in loud arguments with the preachers over scripture. When challenged, she would stand up to anyone and give them a piece of her mind. Her weapon: *words*.

She was very witty, and she used words to defend herself and put arrogant

people in their place. She also used words to defend the cause of African

Americans, who had been enslaved and mistreated all over America, not just

in the South. She made white people aware that black people could express

themselves as clearly as white people. This message did not go over so well, and

she was hated and shouted at and threatened in many of the places she visited.

But wherever she went, she stood up courageously for that most American

tradition: *freedom*. Her specialty: *freedom*

of speech. Without ever using a gun,

Sojourner Truth helped to win

that freedom and others for

future generations of African

Americans — and women.

Clara Barton

(1821–1912)

Most heroes, peaceful or non-peaceful, have both fans and enemies.

What their fans call *heroism*, their enemies might call troublemaking.

There are very few heroes whose heroism is universally appreciated.

+ = CARE

Clara Barton stands out as the greatest example of this kind of heroism.

You see, Clara Barton was a battlefield nurse.

During the American Civil War, Barton volunteered her services as a nurse during the bloodiest battles. Running from patient to patient as cannons roared, her fearlessness and compassion earned her the title "Angel of the Battlefield." With equal care, she tended to soldiers on *both* sides of the war. Saving lives was all that mattered to her, even though it meant risking her own life. Once, as she cradled a wounded soldier in her arms, she felt a flutter on one of her sleeves. Looking down, she saw a bullet hole. Upon looking back to the soldier, she saw that he had just been shot and killed — by the same bullet she had narrowly escaped. Till the day she died, she kept that shirt with the bullet hole. It was a reminder of how close she often came to being killed.

But for Clara Barton, the Civil War was just the beginning of her heroic career. Traveling to Europe, she served as an active-duty member of the Red Cross in a war between Germany and France. The Red Cross was and is a humanitarian health organization that aids people during wars and other disasters. Most important, the Red Cross *does not* take sides. To Clara, it seemed like the perfect organization. Therefore, when she returned to America, she founded the American Red Cross and was its president for twenty years. Even when she was older, in her seventies, Clara still traveled to the sites of disasters to nurse people.

Surrounded by military heroes much of her life, Clara Barton was perhaps even more heroic than they. It is far more heroic to save a life than to take one.

CARE = ✚

Corrie ten Boom

(1892–1983)

From 1933 to 1945, the country of Germany was controlled by the Nazi

Party, whose leader was named Adolph Hitler. Hitler had two main goals:

1) to kill all Jewish people; and 2) to take over the world. In Nazi Germany,

Jewish people were rounded up and put into   boxcars like cattle and then sent to "concentration camps" — places where they were humiliated, tortured, starved, made to do hard labor, then murdered. Hitler believed that Germanic people, or "Aryans," were the "master race" and should rule the world. He believed that Jews, Gypsies, homosexuals, and various other minorities were not even human — and that the world should be "cleansed" of them. Hitler's plan was to take over one country after the next — and *cleanse* them.

In 1940 this evil arrived in Holland, at Corrie ten Boom's doorstep. Hitler invaded her country. Corrie had lived her whole life in Holland, in the peaceful town of Haarlem, and now all she could do was watch as the Nazis took over her streets with their tanks and machine guns. Corrie, who was not Jewish, watched as her Jewish friends were forced to wear the Jewish Star of David on their clothes at all times. She watched as signs went up in windows of stores saying NO JEWS. She watched as rocks were thrown through the windows of Jewish homes, as her non-Jewish neighbors became scared to speak out against this. She watched in horror as Jewish people were marched away by Nazi soldiers, never to be seen again. She felt so helpless!

But Corrie and her family were decent people, and they decided to risk their own lives in order to help as many Jewish people as they could. They turned their house into a hiding place for Jews so the Nazis couldn't take them away to concentration camps. In Corrie's room, there was a bookshelf covering a hole in the wall, and behind that hole was a hidden space, about the size of a closet, where fugitives (mainly Jews) would hide when anyone knocked on their door. Through this method, Corrie and her family saved many lives. Then one night their house was raided by the Nazis. None of the people they were currently hiding were caught. Sadly, Corrie and her family *were* caught. They were all sent to different German prisons and concentration camps, except for Corrie's mother, who had died of illness before the family's arrest. Corrie's father died in a camp, as did her sister Betsie.

Luckily, Corrie did live to tell this amazing story in her book, *The Hiding Place*. During her darkest moments in the Ravensbruck concentration camp, she never stopped trying to remember the human capacity to love other people, even people who hate you and would kill you. This, she claims, and luck, kept her alive, kept her from giving up.

Benito Mussolini, shared this wicked desire. Mussolini was an ally of Hitler. His "Fascist Party" killed and imprisoned a huge amount of Jewish people *and* any non-Jewish people who opposed him — including Ginetta Sagan's parents. When Ginetta Moroni (her original name) was only eighteen years old, her mother, a Jew, was dragged away to a concentration camp . . . where she died. Her father was shot in the street by Fascist soldiers. He was a known member of the Italian Resistance — Italians who resisted the rule of the Fascists by helping Jews escape Italy.

Ginetta was already a member of the Resistance when both her parents were killed. Her role was one that took much courage. Though she was a tiny woman, only 4 feet 11 inches tall, she personally escorted 300 Jews and anti-Fascists across the Italian border into Switzerland, where they would be safe. It was a dangerous journey, and she was finally caught by Fascist soldiers and thrown into a dark cell, where she was tortured for forty-five days. During that time, a prison guard threw her a loaf of bread with a matchbox buried inside. Inside the matchbox was one match and a note. Using the light from the match, Ginetta read the note. It said, "Courage! We're trying to help you." Not long after that, two "guards" pretending to be Nazis dragged her out of her Fascist jail cell — and set her free!

Once she was free, Ginetta Sagan devoted the rest of her life to helping other people around the world — especially victims of torture and unfair imprisonment. Unstoppable, she often assumed different disguises and fake identities to sneak into countries where people were unfairly jailed. In America, where she settled, Ginetta helped to build an organization called Amnesty International. "Amnesty" means *freedom*, and Amnesty International is committed to saving people whose freedom has been taken away. Ginetta started America's first Amnesty International newsletter, which was called *Matchbox* in honor of the matchbox she once received. Her goal was to give unfairly jailed people the same hope she was once given — by writing them letters, by visiting them, and by pressuring their jailers to release them or at least treat them humanely. The symbol of Amnesty International — a candle wrapped in barbed wire — though not created by Ginetta, certainly evokes her own personal symbols: As it so happened, Ginetta carried a piece of barbed wire she'd cut from the fence that once divided Italy and Switzerland. Ginetta Sagan's spirit was like that candle — nothing could put it out.

Abdul Ghaffar Khan

(1890–1988)

In our modern world, Islamic people

are not famous for being peaceful. In

the news, one hears much about

Islamic terrorists and Islamic "holy

war." Islamic leaders are often quoted as

encouraging their people to do great

violence against the Jews and the

"Crusaders" (what Christians are often

called by Islamic leaders).

And yet, it is important to remember that not all Islamic people are violent, not by a long shot. In fact, one of the most peaceful leaders of modern times was Islamic: Abdul Ghaffar Khan. Khan was a deeply religious man, and his Islamic beliefs guided him throughout his life. He believed that Islam was a religion of peace. However, this belief did not stop him from fighting for justice — far from it. Khan devoted his life to helping his people, the Pashtuns. The Pashtuns are an ancient race who live in what is now called Pakistan and Afghanistan. They are also Islamic. And for centuries they have been pushed around by more powerful groups and nations — most notably, Great Britain. Not that long ago, Great Britain conquered and controlled not only India, but Pakistan too.

Inspired by Islam, Khan organized a nonviolent group to defend the rights of Pashtuns against the British colonizers. They were called the "Khudai Khidmatgar." This means the "Servants of God." Because this group believed God to be peaceful, they themselves held only peaceful demonstrations. At one demonstration in 1930,

they were confronted by a platoon of soldiers with raised guns. Rather than run away or attempt to fight the soldiers, these Khidmatgar protesters walked toward the soldiers in orderly lines, slowly and peacefully. The soldiers shot down line after line of the demonstrators until they couldn't stand shooting anymore. Khan's female followers would sometimes lie down in the street holding hands. These sorts of demonstrations enraged the police, who arrested and tortured and executed many of these peaceful people, including Khan, who was imprisoned off and on throughout his life for thirty years, and once for fifteen years straight.

Like Sojourner Truth, Ghaffar Khan traveled by foot from town to town, spreading his dual message of peace and justice. Because he traveled mainly by foot, he rarely made it outside of Pakistan. This might be one reason he is not as famous as his Hindu friend and counterpart, Gandhi, who traveled all over the world. Often called the "Frontier Gandhi," Abdul Ghaffar Khan is a lot more than that. He is perhaps the greatest proof in recent history that Islam can promote peace.

Oscar Romero

(1917~1980)

Like Islam, Catholicism has not always been associated with peace,

historically — especially in the case of the Crusades, a centuries-long

series of military campaigns launched by the Catholic Church. This

being said, there have been some outstanding

Catholic heroes of peace, especially in

modern times. Oscar Romero

is one such hero.

Romero was the Archbishop of El Salvador's Catholic churches. El Salvador

is a very poor Central American country controlled by a military government

and a few rich people. Though it is now run by a democratically elected

government, a few rich people still corner most of the wealth, leaving most

of the country very poor. During Romero's time as Archibishop, 1977–1980,

the military government made life very hard on the nation's poor people.

Back then, underpaid striking workers were often arrested and/or executed

at random, without a trial, without proof that they had done anything wrong.

Originally, Archbishop Romero believed that as a religious leader, it was not

his job to get involved in these sorts of political problems. Then something

happened that changed his mind: One of his priests was murdered by the

Salvadorian police. The priest had been urging El Salvador's poor farmworkers

to band together and demand better wages. After this murder, Romero was

called in to view the priest's body. This was intended as a warning. It was as if

the government was saying *here's what happens to priests who get involved in*

politics, who challenge us. At this moment, an enormous change came over

Romero. He decided to protest what the police had done by shutting down all the churches in El Salvador except his own. The next Sunday, he held a

mass in honor of the slain priest — and thousands of people showed up.

From this point on, Romero dedicated his life to fighting injustice in his

country. He gave strong sermons over the radio denouncing his government.

He asked America to stop giving money to his government. He commanded

the Salvadorian army, in the name of God, to stop killing its own people.

Following the example of Jesus, Romero believed in nonviolence as the only

response to violence.

Archbishop Oscar Romero understood the potential of the Catholic

Church as a beacon of peace and justice — and he turned this understanding

into action.

Paul Rusesabagina

(1954–)

Question: What do you do when something *really* horrible happens, and there are no heroes around to stop the horror?

Answer: You become a hero — especially if your name is Paul Rusesabagina.

Paul Rusesabagina was a hotel manager in the African country of Rwanda. Until the spring of 1994, he was just an average guy, who led a fairly normal life. But that spring, his peaceful life changed abruptly. On April 6, something terrible happened, something so terrible it's hard to explain: The ethnic majority of people in Rwanda, the Hutus, went on a killing spree against the minority group, the Tutsis. Why? The Rwandan government, controlled by Hutus, supplied its Hutu citizens with weapons, commanding them to kill all Tutsis on sight. The government leaders said that the Tutsis were no better than cockroaches and therefore deserved to die. Any Hutu who did not obey this command, said the government leaders, would himself be killed. So, for one hundred days, ordinary people who had been peaceful citizens were now, overnight, transformed into brutal murderers, slaughtering any and all Tutsis they could find — men, women, children . . . next-door neighbors . . . *friends*. . . . It was as if the Hutus had just lost their minds and their humanity.

In the midst of this waking nightmare, Paul Rusesabagina, a Hutu, remained one of the few lights shining in a world that had suddenly turned very, very dark. Not only did Paul refuse to murder his fellow citizens — he turned his hotel into a safe haven for Tutsis, hiding them in various rooms. Day after day, the Hutus repeatedly threatened to kill him and everyone they figured he was hiding. But every time angry Hutus came to the hotel, Paul used his wits to outsmart them, often giving them free drinks to calm them down so they wouldn't kill anyone. Paul's strategy was to keep them talking, to keep them distracted. And it worked! Not a single person hiding out in the hotel was killed.

Using no weapon but his brain, this humble hotel manager put his own life in constant danger to protect other people. The result: He saved 1,268 lives. Amazed to be alive, these survivors were safely transported out of Rwanda.

In the years following the massacre, Paul's heroism became the subject of a movie entitled *Hotel Rwanda*. Paul now lives in Belgium, where he runs the Hotel Rwanda Rusesabagina Foundation, which provides money to children and women in Rwanda and other African nations with similar political problems. About his heroism, he now says, "Being human is a mission of each and everyone. What I have done is what all the people were supposed to have done, so there's no special lesson." In the midst of great evil, Paul Rusesabagina had the courage to remain what he was: a decent human being. And that is a kind of heroism of which we all are capable.

44

Aung San Suu Kyi

(1945~)

Aung San Suu Kyi is a human rights leader in the southeast

Asian country of Burma.* Burma is a country where there

are basically no human rights. What are "human rights"?

* The current military rulers, while ignoring the

will of the people, refer to Burma as "Myanmar."

The author considers this new name illegitimate,

the product of tyranny and lawlessness.

Here are a few, which do not exist in Burma: 1) the right to speak out against the government, 2) the right to choose your own profession, 3) the right to a fair trial if you get arrested by the police, and 4) the right to be treated like a human being by the police. Any Burmese person who demands these rights is either shot by the police or put in jail. Most of these arrests and murders are then covered up, forgotten, and buried.

However, when Aung San Suu Kyi was arrested in 1989 for speaking out against her government, the whole world was watching. You see, she was already famous. Her father was an important general — the George Washington of modern Burma. He helped his country win its independence from England, and in that process he became modern Burma's first political leader. Sadly, he was assassinated before independence was officially achieved. Suu Kyi was only two years old. Little did she know that she would grow up to become a leader too, fighting the same sort of policemen that had killed her father. Unlike him, though, and more like Gandhi, Suu Kyi used peaceful means of combat. Like Gandhi, she would be educated in England. Like Gandhi, she would become a wise and gifted speaker. Like Gandhi, she would be hated by her government. In 1989, she was giving a public speech on human rights, when suddenly the army showed up and pointed their guns straight at her. They had orders to shoot her. Suu Kyi stood her ground and continued speaking. At the last minute, the commanding officer stopped the killing. Nonetheless, a few months later she was put under "house arrest" (jailed in her own house) . . . *for six years*.

During her imprisonment, Suu Kyi was elected prime minister of Burma! But the military dictators who ran the country didn't care who the people elected — they stayed in power and she stayed under arrest. During her imprisonment, she also won the Nobel Peace Prize, which she couldn't leave her country to accept.

Since Suu Kyi was freed in 1995, she has been arrested again and again. And when she is free, the police do everything they can to stop her from speaking publicly, because they know she will speak out against them. Many times, they have filled up the streets surrounding her house with parked cars so she is unable to leave. They have trapped her in her car without food or water for days. Still, she keeps speaking, and writing books too, so that the whole world may know of the injustice in Burma. Rather than leave Burma forever (an option she has been offered repeatedly), Suu Kyi has chosen to remain in Burma, under house arrest, since 2003 — as a way of bringing attention to the injustice of the military government. Aung San Suu Kyi is doing everything she can to make her country a more fair and peaceful place.

silence

Meena
Keshwar
Kamal
(1956–1987)

48

آزادگی

Imagine a world in which women and girls were strongly discouraged from going to school — and schools admitting girls were burned down on a regular basis. In modern day Afghanistan, such a world exists.

Women and girls have basically no human rights in this country. Besides being discouraged from going to school, women are also discouraged from having jobs outside their houses. In Afghanistan, all houses containing females generally have their windows painted black so that no one can see in. When women are outside their homes, they must be covered from head to toe in a "burqa," a black or blue cloth garment with a hood that completely covers the body — except for a tiny hole to breathe and see through. If a woman gets sick, she is not supposed to go to a male doctor. Since almost all the doctors in Afghanistan are men, this means that women generally do not go to *any* doctor when they are sick.

Additionally, Afghani women are discouraged from wearing squeaky or brightly colored shoes. They are discouraged from performing or listening to any music. They are discouraged from watching television or going to the movies. They are discouraged from painting their nails. They are discouraged from laughing. Women who do these things are often beaten, maimed, and murdered.

It has only been *this* bad since the 1990s, when some violent Islamic men called the Taliban took charge of the government and outlawed the aforementioned things. Though the Taliban is no longer officially in charge, and many of their outrageous laws have been abolished, the current government has done little to protect women and girls. Though officially girls are now allowed to go to school, many of their schools are being burned down on a regular basis by the Taliban (which still wields enormous power). Many teachers, students, and parents live in such fear that they would rather shut down these schools than risk them being burned down.

Back in the 1970s, Afghani women *were* allowed to go to school, and they did not have to cover themselves from head to toe. However, they did not have equal rights to men. This bothered an Afghani woman named Meena Keshwar Kamal. So, at the age of twenty, in 1977, Meena started an organization to help women in both Afghanistan and the neighboring Islamic country, Pakistan. The organization she started is called RAWA, or the Revolutionary Association of the Women of Afghanistan. Its purpose was to provide girls and women with good education and health care. Meena knew that she was putting her life in danger through daring to help women in a country like Afghanistan, and she ultimately sacrificed her life for this cause.

But even after Meena's death in 1987, RAWA lives on. To this day, it provides education and health care to Afghani and Pakistani women and girls — all in secret, though. In Afghanistan, there are now dozens of secret schools and orphanages, all for girls, being run in RAWA members' houses. These teachers, doctors, and nurses, at the risk of their own lives, are working to create a better future for Afghani women and girls.

52

Marla Ruzicka
(1977–2005)

Modern-day

Iraq has been a

war zone, off and on, ever since

the first American-led invasion.

In 1991, America invaded Iraq, in

response to Iraq's invasion of its

neighbor, Kuwait. In 2003, America led another military invasion of Iraq in order to remove Saddam Hussein, Iraq's dictator, from power. Under Saddam Hussein, Iraqi people had very few freedoms. They were not allowed to speak out against him. Those who did were imprisoned or executed. Certain ethnic groups in Iraq, like the Kurds, were regularly executed by Hussein's army. Very few people would disagree that Saddam Hussein was a terrible leader. However, many people disagree over whether or not America should have invaded Iraq to remove him from power. America has had very little support from other countries. Most people in other countries think that America has done more harm than good in Iraq. However, there are still many Americans who believe that the American army has helped the Iraqi people. They believe that American soldiers have risked and sacrificed their lives for Iraqi freedom.

One thing is for certain: In any war, innocent people are going to get hurt — people who are just going about their daily lives. Even army generals say that this is unavoidable. In Iraq, hundreds of thousands of innocent people have been injured and killed. And there are certain Americans who have devoted their lives to helping these innocent victims. One such American is Marla Ruzicka.

In 2001, Marla Ruzicka was a twenty-four-year-old, blonde-haired Californian woman who was deeply upset by the suffering caused by war. She decided to turn her feelings into action when she went to

Afghanistan to help innocent victims

of the war that was happening there. In

2003, she shifted her efforts to the even more

dangerous war zone which was Iraq. With no gun to protect her,

with nothing but her sunny California smile, Marla went door

to door in Iraq, to see who had been hurt by the war. With an

Iraqi translator, she was able to talk to people, hear their stories, and find out who

had been killed, injured, and lost. And she did this as bullets flew past her. . . .

   As she collected this information, she reported it to people in the United

States government. With the help of Senator Patrick Leahy, she was able to get

twenty million dollars in aid for these innocent Iraqi victims and their families.

Working with the American army, she made sure that this money was distributed

to the right people. Working with reporters, she made sure that the stories of

these Iraqi people did not get lost.

   Marla Ruzicka knew the risks of being in Iraq — just as a soldier knows the

risks of war. Her life, brief as it was, is a monument to selflessness.

William
Feehan
(1929–2001)

56

William (Bill) Feehan had always wanted to be a fireman. His father had

been a fireman, and Bill knew that this was the life for him too. So, in 1959,

he joined the New York City  Fire Department — the biggest American fire department in the biggest American city. And he immediately

loved it — he loved fighting fires!

He loved rushing into burning buildings and saving people. Bill didn't know why

he loved this — he just did. Firefighting is a job for brave people who aren't afraid of

danger, who risk their own lives to save other people. And Bill Feehan showed such

bravery as a fireman that he was promoted again and again — all the way up to the

highest post in the entire New York City Fire Department.

Feehan loved working for the Fire Department so much that when he reached

the retirement age of sixty-five, he decided *not* to retire. *Why retire?* he thought. What

on earth would he do in *retirement?* So Feehan stayed on and on and on. At the age of

seventy-one, though, he was no longer putting out fires. Instead, now being the deputy

commissioner, he worked a desk job. If there was a major fire, it was

his job to tell other firemen how to deal with it. But he always

kept his turnout coat and helmet in the trunk of his

car, just in case the day arrived when he might

be able to swing into action once again.

Little did Feehan know, when he

woke up on the morning of

September 11, 2001, that day had arrived. . . .

Just before 9:00 A.M., after hearing that an airplane had crashed into a building, Feehan's assistant called him over to the window, where they saw something terrible: Black smoke was pouring out of a big gaping hole in one of the twin towers of the World Trade Center, the two tallest skyscrapers in New York City. So Feehan did what any true-blue fireman would do: He rushed to the scene of the fire. By the time the seventy-one-year-old deputy commissioner got there, grabbing his helmet and turnout coat, a second plane had crashed into the other World Trade Center tower. This was no accident, but a deliberate act of violence — an act of terrorism! While everyone was running for their lives, scrambling to get away from the burning buildings, Feehan and all the other firemen were trying to get in, to save people trapped by fire. As they were doing this, something sickening happened: First one tower collapsed . . . and then the other . . . killing many, many people, many of whom were firemen, including . . . Bill Feehan.

Firemen, like Bill Feehan, clean up messes. Like emergency workers, they save lives. They risk their own lives. That's their job. And they do this job with no hope of ever being famous. For this reason, they are perhaps the most selfless of all peaceful heroes. What would we do without them?

Library of Congress Cataloging-in-Publication Data

Winter, Jonah.   Peaceful heroes / by Jonah Winter; illustrated by Sean Addy. — 1st ed.   p.   cm.
ISBN 978-0-439-62307-0 (hardcover : alk. paper)   1. Heroes—Biography—Juvenile literature.
2. Peace—History—Juvenile literature.   I. Addy, Sean, ill. II. Title.   CT107.W66 2009   920.02—dc22   2008048311

ISBN-13: 978-0-439-62307-0   ISBN-10: 0-439-62307-3
10 9 8 7 6 5 4 3 2   15 16 17 18 /0
First edition, September 2009   Printed in Malaysia 108

The display type was set in P22 Vincent and various other fonts. The text type was set in Hoefler Text.
The art for this book was created using oil and acrylic and collage. Book design by Marijka Kostiw

To
Mills
Crosland,
a
peaceful hero
of mine.

— J.W.

To my wife, Tonya,
Wayne and Chris,
Jen and Jimmy
and Foof.
Great parents and my
"Peaceful Heroes."

— S.A.